CW01508005

Faith In Humanity

How We Can Learn To Get Along

by
John Scott Burquin

to Paula

Contents

Foreword...1

Chapter 1 - Stand-Alone Passages................19

Chapter 2 - Don't Lie....................................27

Chapter 3 - Non-Oppression.......................31

Chapter 4 - Don't Steal................................35

Chapter 5 - Keeping Vows...........................37

Chapter 6 - Don't Judge...............................41

Chapter 7 - Do Not Kill................................45

Chapter 8 - The "Don'ts".............................51

Chapter 9 - The "Do's" Part One.................55

Chapter 10 - The "Do's" Part Two...............63

Chapter 11 – Peace......................................67

Chapter 12 - Keep To Yourself....................69

Epilogue...71

Foreword:

My wife is a better person than me. Even when she has to deal with angry, difficult, mean-spirited people, she looks for one good thing in them. She looks for that one glimmer of commonality or grace in order to deal patiently with them and not let their negativity affect her. She looks for a redeemable quality and then focuses on that aspect of them. It's a gift. It is also the point of this book.

*****

Nineteen people decide to run two airplanes into buildings in 2001. They are described as Muslim. The Muslim religion unfairly begins to be synonymous with terrorism. A man goes on a killing spree in Norway, leaving over seventy people dead. He is described as a Christian. His stated goal was to save Norway from a Muslim takeover. Through an act of terrorism. I heard a radio program the other day that was running vintage 1970s news stories. One covered the Israeli-Palestinian conflict. It sounded identical to and indistinguishable from, any news story coming from that area today. There are considerably more examples that could be given. Historically, monotheists eliminated the polytheist competition, there were the Crusades, and the Muslim conquests starting in the 7th century, the list is long. Now? Just check your daily news source. Which leads me to this question: What is wrong with us?

For the past two years, I have read through the Old Testament, the Quran, and the New Testament, in that order. One reason is that I've encountered people from each of these viewpoints who see little to no value in the other two views. People have their own belief and see no reason to explore where other people are coming from in their beliefs. I think subconsciously, or maybe even consciously, they also feel that they don't want the possibility of their beliefs getting tainted or challenged; it's an existential threat. For a Christian to read the Quran can be anathema to some, as an example. It is for exactly this reason, the shutting out of other's opinions, this disdain toward another's belief system, a dismissal of a whole group of people as unworthy of consideration, that I put this book together. Because we have to have a better approach to each other.

And honestly, our differences are so much smaller and can be seen that way in scale if we step back and expand our view. The difference between Judaism and Christianity is that Christians accept Jesus as messiah and personal savior. Jesus is not a part of Jewish theology, therefore the Hebrew Bible, by definition, does not include the New Testament. Jesus is not considered a divine being by the Jewish faith, but is seen as a teacher. Christians believe in the Trinity – the Father, the Son, and the Holy Ghost; Muslims do not. Muslims believe Jesus to be a messenger of God, not the Son of God. Muslims have Muhammad as their prophet touchstone; Jews and Christians do not. Others might quibble that it's more complicated than that, but really, that's it. And while these differences divide how people worship, they shouldn't divide people.

Islam and Christianity both reference the Old Testament. Fundamentally, Jews, Muslims, and Christians all worship the same God. They come about it from different angles, but as the saying goes, there's more than one way to load a dishwasher. The way you do it is right for you. Not necessarily right for someone else. Neither should it matter to you how your neighbor loads their dishwasher.

I was curious what all of the fuss was about. The world seems to spend an inordinate amount of time talking about, discussing, arguing, praying, meeting, fighting, congregating, writing, and reading about religion. And I don't mean to ignore the Eastern religions, the Buddhists, the Taoists, the Hindus, and the many, many, many, many, many other religious viewpoints. This conversation isn't meant to be a balanced representation of all religions and their positives and negatives. I'm concentrating on the three main ones that, at least in my narrow spectrum of the world, seem to create a lot of discord, either separately or in how they treat each other - Judaism, Islam, and Christianity. The Big Three. Though, again, in numbers, there are more Hindu and

Buddhist adherents than those in the Judaic faith.

I embarked on this journey because I felt an obligation to have an informed opinion. Being American, we can't help but be inundated with the Christian view. Growing up I could read in almost any doctor's office the stories from both the Old and New Testament simplified for children with accompanying water-color illustrations. I attended a couple of churches throughout life but none for a sustained length of time. On every block I drive, there are churches every hundred yards - Baptist, Presbyterian, Catholic - pick one. I'm surrounded by Christians, both the quiet, reserved ones and the more vocal, abrasive ones.

In the United States, the majority profess some variety of Christian viewpoint and in some strange twist of logic are very loud in expressing that they are persecuted everywhere they look. Though this country is based on, in part and theory, the acceptance of everyone and their religions, a lot of professedly religious individuals come across as very intolerant. Certainly post-9/11 this intolerance has only escalated. It's a shame. The dichotomy of this country has always piqued my interest, where on one side you get a heavy dose of one religious view and on the other side you have a philosophy of being open-minded to different views; after all, we have offered ourselves up as the repository for the "others" of the world, something many forget is our greatest strength.

The beginnings of the country were from those fleeing religious persecution. To then turn around and stake a majority claim in order to suppress or keep other religions out is wrong. I don't wish to come across as singling out one particular religion; it's just that Christianity is the main one I've been exposed to, with its positive verbal message and its warts as well. Religion is fine - it seems like the people that muck it up.

Up to now, my appreciation of these three religions was ankle-deep. Not being around the Jewish religion, a lot of my exposure was through popular culture, news, and history. The Islamic religion even less. I also questioned whether the stories that I had picked up through life about Christianity were accurate. I wanted to change that limitation and also see if what I hear from others had any validity.

In Western Civilization, I don't see a lot of people doing their due diligence and investigating or appreciating other people's points of view. Rather they seek out things that reinforce their belief, whether it's something that positively reinforces their religion or negatively reinforces their view of other religious practices. And the pronouncements I've heard from Religion A against Religion B often come across at least as condescending and dismissive, very often ignorant. It almost seems as if people are frightened of having their beliefs challenged, as if a questioning mind is a threat. On the one hand, it should not be necessary to vilify another religion for you to feel comfortable practicing the spirituality that works for you. On the other hand, I would think that if your belief is sufficiently strong, it should be able to withstand seeing what other religions are about. If you reject the notion of understanding where another person is coming from, then you forfeit the right to comment on them, because you'd only be doing so from a point of ignorance and your opinion is invalid.

One skill human-beings excel at is in group-identifying. There is a biological benefit to doing this, but our population is expanding at the same time that the world is shrinking in the sense of how much easier it is to affect one another. I don't think I'm going out on a limb too much to say that the majority of, say, Christians, have not read the Quran. And, to be fair, how many Muslims have read the New Testament? Not many, I'm sure. They all have an opinion, often negative, about each other. And these are usually based on the shallowest and most superficial of interpretations. If anyone does read or know something about another religion, it's those easily parsed out verses that put the most negative spin or reinforces the already negative assumptions. This is not constructive. And that's what's vexing, because each of these religions espouses peaceful coexistence and love; just not for each other, apparently, in practice.

Being a layman, I wanted to understand where the

various opposing views come from. Maybe it's the way information is presented or promoted that makes it look like these three groups are always at odds, but I don't think so. Certainly, the worst of a group that creates the most clamor are the ones going to make the news, possibly overshadowing the more thoughtful and accepting people within that group. I'd like to think that the majority of people within each religion look disdainfully at their vocal, destructive, and intolerant counterparts. And yet, if the moderate ones are the majority, I don't hear those same people condemning or correcting the vocal ones in equal measure. If members of Religion A insult or attack Religion B, I don't see moderate voices in Religion A telling them they've gone too far or what they're doing is wrong and not representative of Religion A's outlook. It's as if to group-identify is more important than doing right by each other as human beings, our basic commonality. Or perhaps, among many, there's an agreement that, hey, even though a member of Religion A thinks it's wrong that we bombed Religion B, well, you know, those Religion B people do weird stuff and things we don't agree with, so it's not viewed as completely bad. Which is a shame because the loud and rude cast a pall over any appreciation of the positive aspects of a shared religion. And when you combine ignorant with vocal, then a general aversion to a particular religion can set in.

I understand there are historical and cultural issues at play here as well in these altercations. However, religion still seems to be the motivating, self-perpetuating force behind even those misunderstandings and ingrained animosities. Perhaps, also, it's a question of how the majority (of anything - gender, ethnicity, color, etc.) treats a minority. Christians may feel comfortable thinking, speaking, and doing ill to Muslims in America. In Muslim countries, certainly Christians and Jews are persecuted. Not a problem of religion, but a problem as to how human beings historically treat minority populations. Which gets back to the point of this book because religion tells us how to treat each other better. When religion is used as an excuse to be intolerant of minority populations, it does not benefit their religion to do so and is, as you'll see in this book, the exact opposite of what their scripture advocates.

Human beings are very good at seeing differences in each other. Christianity is fractionated over 1,000 different sects. Islam has three major divisions and dozens of sub-denominations. Judaism is the same way. That's how little *they* can even agree amongst themselves. What I wanted to do (and when I started I wasn't sure if it would be possible) was to find, through their own writings, where the Big Three could agree. Can we agree to disagree on some things and tone down the intensity? I don't know. But what I wanted to do was get past the disagreements, whether you believe Jesus was just a man and a good prophet or whether he was the Son of God or whether you find it wrong to attribute a son to God for example. I wanted to get past the rituals and the different story interpretations that muddy up the waters and allow for misunderstandings. It's easy to disagree. It's easy to be disagreeable.

But, where can we agree?

I did also put a slant on what we could agree on generally as human beings, not just those who describe themselves as spiritual or religious. Because when you identify yourself as a particular religious follower, you pigeonhole yourself in how other people perceive you. Just as you might pigeonhole someone else when you hear their religious view. Right or wrong, this is a natural process that people go through. Yet, there is always more to a person than just their religion. I kept that in mind as well during my readings. That's also the point I said I'd get back to. I'm wanting people to be as open-minded as possible in reading this book. To identify myself with a particular religion would automatically color, for certain groups of people, their response to what I'm trying to accomplish here. I like to joke that I practice Egalitarianism and let the other person figure out what that means. I would like this to be accepted for the earnest plea that it is. That if we do not learn how to get along, then we're just creating our own hell on earth and, at a minimum, not abiding by what we report to be in our belief systems.

I'd like to clarify one objection people may have to this. A lot of people will bring up opposing religions' teachings and writings and point out their negative aspects or the hypocrisies or the contradictions. They'll say that Religion A professes peace, but look what it says here about violence in their text! Again, that is not the point of this exercise. If we want to find out where other religions, or individuals thereof, purportedly drop the ball, there are plenty of people out there willing and able to do so. My point here is to be the person who brings up the positive relationships that religions share. I don't want to be part of the "Yes, but...." crowd or the "What they say isn't true" crowd. We all need to realize that each religion has an aspect to it that we can agree on, regardless of other perceptions. It's that one good thing my wife looks for in others.

I had no preconceived notions as to how this would turn out. I truly remained open to whatever I read, with the only caveat being in looking at each verse, section, chapter with the thought, "Can we ALL agree on what this says?", whether you are religious or non-religious. What does each of these religions, stripped down, have to say about forming a positive relationship with each other? Leaving aside opinions that I formed during my reading journey, I was surprised at how little, of the hundreds and hundreds of pages, I ended up setting aside as meeting the criteria. However, the heart weighs less than a pound and is the driving force for your entire body. Perhaps, this core of material is the heart of humanity.

I'm sure that some people will find my abridged renderings here as blasphemous or irreverent in some manner, but I would like those people to take a moment and understand that I don't mean what I've done here to be some kind of replacement for one or all of these religions or dismissive of the other aspects of their beliefs. I do not intend this to be a comprehensive analysis and admittedly do not come from a scholarly background. I'm sure there might be some academicians who can point out pertinent things that I should have included. I am human after all. I simply wanted to put forward a list of things that anyone could look at (whether you're a Muslim, Jew, Christian, an atheist, agnostic, Eastern religion practitioner, or undecided) and agree on. There has to be a starting point. And we should always proceed from the point of agreeing on certain things first.

For instance, I think some people don't realize that these three branches of religion are all worshipping the same God, just in their own way. I've heard some Christians use a dismissive tone when talking about Allah, as if they were referencing a different deity, rather than a language interpretation issue. It's not a competition. It's not a matter of who's "right" and who's "wrong". Everyone seems so hell-bent (yeah, that's right, I said it) to be right that they forget how to act right. Taking a lesson that all three religions do, at least in theory, agree about - leave it to God to sort out.   Unfortunately, I don't see many people practicing this. They seem to want to take an active role in separating out which is the better religion, who are the better people. As if God needs our help. Back to the dishwasher analogy.   Everyone loads the dishwasher differently.   There's no reason to fight about the "right" way to do it. All the dishes get cleaned anyway.

One thing that surprised me during this journey was, within the few things that I set aside as agreeable was how much overlap there was. To hear people compare religions or talk about their own or give their opinions on other religions, you would think that these were entirely different worlds they're talking about.   As you'll see, there are quite a few commonalities between them. Some universal truths so to speak. I wonder how surprising it would be to Religious Person A to see that Religion B says a lot of the   same   things   Religion   A   does?

In some cases I have used the exact passages, in others, I have paraphrased for clarity.   Also, sometimes I have abbreviated a passage in trying to get to the meaning of it since some verses can be a bit verbose. The other acknowledgment I need to make is how everyone references the Old Testament. Sure, they seem to pick and choose from it, but Christianity and Islam are so-called late-comers to the party, and they build from the foundation of the Old Testament. That's also why I would like to point out that if one of the branches of religion doesn't seem to have a specific "don't *something*" or "do *something*" verse, it's not because they think it's ok or not ok, it's more likely because they honor that verse or idea from a different text or I have not been as diligent as I think in presenting the ideas.

Finally, I thought that as a human being I should do my part to try to sort out the discord. I have a deep-seated self-interest in seeing people and the world get along. There's way too much negativity out there, and I was hoping, in my small way, to point out some things that we can agree on and seek more positively in each other. I would hope (there's that word again) that, if people could emphasize the positive attributes that can be found in scripture, our shared humanity, lead with those, and deemphasize the differences, perhaps.....perhaps we could all get along better. We should all notice that, first, we are human beings and have much more in common than differences. We all have wants and needs, limitations and strengths, aspirations for our children, and goals for ourselves. We bump up against each other in achieving these, which is normal when you share a finite space, regardless of how large the Earth seems. This shouldn't allow the normal everyday life-jostling result in bruising each other or causing us to strike out at another. Up to this point we have been like children, tromping on each other without regard to others' feelings, putting our selfishness first. And I understand how prior encounters may have generated animosity and grudges. However, if we are to be better than children, we have to pick a point where we treat each other better. Where we put past grudges and disdain behind us and decide, moving forward, to be more tolerant of differences. It may be frustrating at times, but we have no choice but to share this planet, folks.

Because religion is such a sensitive subject for people, I would like to say this one last time. What I am offering here is but a simple plea from one human being on this planet, earnestly hoping to open up a conversation to enable us all to get along better. I doubt my thoughts here are particularly brilliant. I have just tried to use the writings that are readily available to everyone and are referenced by many, writings that are familiar and used by a great many people, to perhaps see each other in a friendlier light. I hope the reader finds this enlightening.

There's a great quote from an unlikely source, but it stuck in my twelve-year-old brain when I heard it. In *Oh, God*, the George Burns movie, John Denver's character, Jerry, is imploring Burns' God to work some magic and fix the world's problems. He replies, "I gave you a world and everything in it." Jerry replies, "But we need help!" Then God says, "That's why I gave you each other."

The Ten Commandments
An example of approach

If you need reminding, here's the short, EZ form:

1. You shall have no other gods before Me.
2. You shall not make idols.
3. You shall not take the name of the LORD your God in vain.
4. Remember the Sabbath day, to keep it holy.
5. Honor your father and your mother.
6. You shall not murder.
7. You shall not commit adultery.
8. You shall not steal.
9. You shall not bear false witness against your neighbor.
10. You shall not covet.

I want to spend just a little time on this to address questions as to why not all of the Ten are represented in the subsequent pages and also to elucidate more clearly my thought processes. I pick the Ten Commandments as a point of discussion mainly because everyone knows these (or is that my own upbringing bias showing?). These are the ones foremost in people's mind when it comes to scripture. The Big Ten are the ones that everyone gets riled up about if they're placed in a government facility, for instance. They get a lot of attention.

The first, second, and third are not included here because they are not germane to how we treat one another.   As above, the first commandment is followed by all of the Big Three religions anyway. The Sabbath day (number 4) is not one people can agree on and, again, doesn't impinge on the way we interact with each other. Sometimes number 4 can be a point of divisiveness with people judging others if they are "breaking the Sabbath".   Again, we're all about inclusiveness and agreeability, not things that obstruct. How one person celebrates the Sabbath and when should not impinge on how someone else does or does not do it. Also, I couldn't help thinking that all football players break number 4 on a regular basis and we cheer them on.

Honoring your father and mother (number 5) is easy if they've done their job correctly. But it is not absolute. There are some bad and some very bad parents out there that, at a minimum, do not deserve honoring. So. Not included. My bias? Sure. My book.

Number 10 about coveting is an individual mandate. It is about feeling, not action. Coveting that turns into stealing is a bad thing, yet coveting in and of itself is a personal attribute that I'm pretty sure no human being is capable of not doing. We can control our actions and what we say, but controlling individual aspects of our emotional spectrum is a bit much to ask. We can be angry about something someone did, and we can even choose to express it, it's how we go about doing that that makes a difference in interpersonal relationships.

That's the crux of what I'm trying to get at. You can disagree with someone and let it go. You can disagree with someone and tell them your point of view while still being true to your belief and not insulting them. However, when you disagree with someone, and you badger them, throw things at them, insist they're wrong, destroy their property, kill them, speak ill of them - these are not the actions that scripture condones.

Before anyone gets upset, please understand that if you hold the tenth commandment dearly to your heart, then please feel free to continue to do so. Continue not to covet. Religion is a very personal thing and how you go about it should always be important to your emotional and spiritual makeup. I am not saying people shouldn't follow it. I am not advocating for you to change one thing about your belief. It's just for this discussion of how we treat each other; there are some things that will not be brought up if only to not muddy the conversational waters. The other aspects of the Big Ten get their due attention later. This concludes my hopefully helpful aside regarding the Big Ten and my thought processes.

Chapter One
Stand-alone passages

Genesis - Chapter 41 - Joseph's wisdom of saving up food during good times to get through the lean years of famine.

Genesis - Chapter 45 - Joseph emphasizing the good that came of something bad – his brothers sold him into slavery, mainly due to their jealousy of him, and yet, because they did, he found himself in a position to advise how to avoid famine and therefore helped many people

Exodus - Chapter 22 – Many examples are given but, generally, make restitution when someone has done someone else wrong even accidentally.

Exodus - Chapter 23 - Don't follow a mob. Help an animal even if it belongs to your enemy.

Leviticus - Chapter 5 - Come forward if you have information about a crime.

Deuteronomy - Chapter 5 - Don't commit adultery.

Deuteronomy - Chapter 27 - Don't take a bribe to harm an innocent.

These passages generally stood on their own and did not have the repetition that we see for a lot of the later verses and chapters to come. I don't know if that's because these were mostly sensible things and it was felt that they didn't need the constant drum-beat repetitive examples or not.

Story-wise, Joseph was the only one that seemed to have a worthwhile lesson for everyone. Yes, I'm aware of all of the cautionary tales that say "listen to God" and "don't forget to do such and such", but those were both ubiquitous and often covered in other areas. Also, most people agree on worshipping God a lot; it's in the specifics they tend to disagree which is why they aren't included here. In the spirit of finding those universal agreements, Joseph was the only one that made the grade; his were novel lessons. I particularly liked the positive spin he put on his brothers selling him into slavery. Here was someone who took an egregious action done to them by others and saw only the good that came of it, even to the point or reassuring his brothers when they realized their wrong. If we could all look at our circumstances, especially in the worst of times, and only see the positive, the world would be a better place.

Making restitution, or accepting responsibility, is something our legal system seems always to have to enforce. The legal system is man-made, with all of its faults, and is an imperfect way of enforcing behavior. How much better would it be if people followed the basic principle of owning up to what they did wrong and trying to make it right without being forced to do so legally? Not even necessarily because God is watching, but just because it's right.

I'd like to extrapolate on the mob issue. I think avoiding group-think is important. I also think that's one of the fundamental problems with organized religions; there's a tendency to nod at everything someone says as long as they're part of your group. It's what allows the vociferous fringe dwellers leeway to say whatever they want as long as once in a while they link up what they say to scripture in some manner. No one wants to correct them or ask them to tone it down because "some" of the things are what the group agrees with and people don't want to be singled out from the group as being adversarial, even if in a moderate, conciliatory way. It's fine if everyone is following the positive edicts and advice. However, when the negative, ugly side rears up with unfavorable opinions regarding other groups of people, those religious followers nodding and agreeing lend credence to the crazies amongst them to take matters into their own hands. The fact that no one says anything near like "That may be true, however.......let's not kill them" (for example) is unfortunate. It gives cover to the extremists even if that was not the intention of the majority. The shades of intolerance in a religion toward others should not be encouraged. A lot of advice in scripture is to put each other first and provide positive stop-gaps that are supposed to get people to think, first, how to do right. Following a mob is the direct antithesis of this, and every congregant needs to be cognizant of this possibility. Everyone needs to think for themselves. One of the reasons I think we have the problems and misunderstandings between the Big Three is that we all cloister and hunker-down in our conclaves of agreement. Christians don't attend Synagogues, Muslims don't attend Catholic services, Jews don't go to Mosques, etc. It's no wonder we can't see each other; we're all purposefully isolated from one another. That's what makes it easy to villainize each other. It's also what nefarious groups, with their agendas, within these conclaves use to get one group to hate another group.

The helping an animal out of a ditch even if it's your enemy's property I believe is supposed to mean more than that specific situation. First off, if we all followed the positive edicts within this book, we wouldn't have enemies; a lot of scripture tangentially acknowledges this unfortunate reality. Past that naïve, positive thinking, however, it's a nice thought not to take out aggression on an innocent animal just because it belongs to someone you don't like. This can be extrapolated to other property or to friends and relatives of your enemy. It's also proactive. You're supposed to help. You're not even allowed to just walk on by and ignore the problem through passive neglect. To do right, you must help, regardless of who you are helping in the process.

(Full disclosure, it says "sin" not "crime", but since scripture can be vague and opaque, it's a simple interpretation to talk about crime or someone having wronged another.) Hard to believe that we must be told by a higher power to come forward if we have information about a crime. People get scared though and worry about repercussions, so this is supposed to be God's way of gently prodding. Again, have you noticed that scripture assumes that a bunch of people aren't going to pay attention to its recommendations? Because if everyone abided, then there really wouldn't be a crime would there? We wouldn't even need such prodding as these verses give. We are not allowed to stay silent if we know something. Staying silent equals complicity or even agreement. Again, it requires action on our part.

Don't commit adultery; number 7 on the Top Ten chart. This is a trust issue. Trust between people. I don't think anyone can disagree on this one and it needs no further discussion. It's an understood truth. It's one of the big "don'ts".

Don't take a bribe to harm an innocent. Another one that flabbergasts me that we have to have this explained to us. It seems like we skipped a step too.

Because no one should be harming an innocent in the first place. This brings up the tangential status of others not involved in the direct harming of someone. You shouldn't take a bribe to look the other way or to set someone up. And if you know of the crime about to come, you need only look a couple of paragraphs back to see what the right thing to do is. I'm never sure if my upbringing caused these lessons just to seep in, but I'm amazed that scripture felt the need to put down what seems to be pretty basic rules of behavior toward each other. These seem self-evident to me. If they don't seem self-evident to someone else, will they change that person's behavior? Will someone read and look at such lessons and think, "Wow. I've been doing things wrong all this time!"

*****

In Victoria, Texas, a Victoria Islamic Centre was burned down. Previously, the mosque had been broken into. The Jewish people of the community presented a key to their synagogue to one of the mosque's founders so that they could use it for their worship. Robert Loeb, the president of Temple Bnai Israel said, "When a calamity like this happens, we have to stand together." Children from a local Catholic school visited and presented the Muslim community with a tree, which will be planted on the grounds of the new mosque in a "spirit of love where the cross hugs the crescent."

*****

A minority Christian community in Gaza provided aid and shelter to 1,200 Muslim refugees.

*****

During World War II, Muslims in Kosovo and Albania saved many Jews from the Nazis in the German-occupied territory.

Chapter Two

Exodus - Chapter 20 – You shall not bear false witness against your neighbor.

Leviticus - Chapter 6 - Don't lie about things trusted to you. Don't lie or support someone else's lie.

Deuteronomy - Chapter 5 - You shall not bear false witness against your neighbor.

Deuteronomy - Chapter 27 - Don't move your neighbor's landmark.

Surah Al-Baqarah - 042 - Don't lie.

Matthew - Chapter 15 - Don't lie.

Colossians - Chapter 3 - Do not lie to one another.

This is a big one. This one gets repeated a lot, and all of the Big Three agree about it. It even tries to close off loopholes, because you would think just saying, "Don't lie about anything." would be sufficient. Scripture brings up other situations and makes sure that the reader understands that the "don't lie" edict applies everywhere. Two areas that weren't covered specifically, however, are 1) lying to yourself and 2) passing on a lie that you don't know is a lie. These two exceptions, however, make me think that it is deliberate lying that is prohibited. Knowledgeable lying. Like moving your neighbor's landmark - a form of lying where you know exactly what you're doing is wrong. I will admit that as clear as this seems, I wasn't sure whether it was something everyone could agree on. Because we all lie in some manner throughout a typical day. We don't tell someone exactly how we feel when asked. We tell our significant other that outfit looks nice on them because it's obvious to us that they like it and would take umbrage otherwise. We make up Santa Claus and the Easter Bunny for the children - a lie we all get caught at eventually.

The saying goes that we are all heroes of our own stories. We weave our personal histories to reflect on us in the best possible way. However, we must beware of lying to ourselves to justify actions against other people. Not only religious teachings, but just plain human kindness, should make us bear responsibility for our actions. One shouldn't lie to themselves that persecuting another group is religiously justified and God's will. This book specifically points out that is not the point of scripture. One needs to be honest with themselves and cannot use religion as cover for their intolerance.

I'd like to talk briefly about the aspect of passing on

a lie you don't know is a lie, because I feel this is another source, especially in the fast-paced information age that feeds people's perceptions of each other, more often than not, negatively.

"A lie can travel halfway around the world before the truth can get its shoes on."

"If you repeat a lie often enough, people will believe it, and you will even come to believe it yourself."

We need to be very careful when it comes to passing the information we receive on to others. When we talk amongst like-minded people, there's a trust issue that can cloud judgment. We need to be wary of gossip and propaganda. The people telling you an untruth may not even be aware it is not true; it may not be intended maliciously. However, these kinds of things can have consequences. Don't blindly accept something as fact just because it fits some preconceptions you may have. Facts should always be checked. One, it keeps you intellectually honest. Two, it stops the viral effect of perpetuating a lie. The Jewish people have had hundreds of years of persecution and deaths because of the anti-Semitic accusation and falsehood that they use the blood of Christian children in their rituals. We need to avoid the 21st century version of such atrocities. The problem with thinking poorly of others and passing on lies about them is that eventually, your group will be on the receiving end.

There's lying to protect someone too. Lying to

protect a bad person, say your brother who robbed a bank, is wrong, regardless of familial loyalty. However, lying to Nazis about whether you are secretly housing Jews is a whole different level and is certainly commendable. The main reason I kept it in though is, of course, as a people we can all agree that lying is not a good practice, but there are occasions it is used. And the lying that we all agree on as egregious enough is the level of lying that causes trouble for others. That deep-seated lying that you really can't pass off as having been anything other than intending harm to another or a way to avoid punishment for something you've done wrong.

Chapter Three

Exodus - Chapter 22 - Don't do wrong or oppress a stranger.

Leviticus - Chapter 19 – You shall not oppress your neighbor.

Surah An-Nisa - 036 – Do good to neighbors who are strangers, the companion by your side, the wayfarer you meet. Be good to orphans and the poor.

Zechariah - Chapter 7 - Oppress not the widow, nor the fatherless, the stranger, nor the poor.

Sum totaled, don't wrong or oppress anyone. On any individual or race/cultural basis. Do not wrong them by word or deed is implied. Interestingly, there's no action given to actively help others, though the Quran *suggests* doing good. Whereas other verses prompted an action on the part of the follower, this is more of a passive thing. I think this is enlightening. It's telling people to let other people be who and what they are or want to be. It's saying to not "actively" oppress someone else. Leave them alone. Let them be.

I've been introduced to the concept that if Religious Person A tolerates another person who violates a Religious A precept, that it is the same as condoning it and therefore puts the onus on the religious person to correct or castigate them, otherwise it reflects poorly on them and in somehow God will judge them negatively. This is a convoluted way to justify intolerance. How someone else is acting or going about their life is their responsibility. If it is not harming others or that Religious Person A in particular, it should not be anyone else's business. Religious members need to stop trying to be humanity's enforcers. That has been one of the bigger reasons, historically, of causing friction between people. Your religion is simply that. Yours. If it helps you in life, I am happy for you. How someone else is finding their way through life is not your problem or responsibility.

I think, in part, this may be a broad interpretation of Leviticus Chapter 5 about informing on those who "sin" or as it is also interpreted as "crime". First off, "sin" is between an individual and their God. One person's "sin" is not another person's "sin". It may be a sin for someone to eat certain meats or not abide by certain rituals according to their religion. However, whether they do or do not abide by those edicts, if they do not harm or affect others, that is on them and their individual conscience. It is not for others, especially those of a different religion, to correct or oppress them. How one practices their own religion or goes about their life is no one else's business.

A "crime", however, is a different thing. By definition, this is something that does negatively affect others, whether through theft, lies, or bodily harm. As a society there are things that we identify as crimes. All people, but religious people in general, need to not confuse or conflate the terms "sin" and "crime". This only causes problems between people.

A lot of the evil done by people is in not just living their own lives but in pushing their opinions on others; enforcing restrictions and limitations on other people. This is the definition of oppression. When you feel like you have something to say about how someone else lives, just remember that God can take care of things. You don't need to be involved. You only need worry about your own relationship with God. Later we will get around to the Golden Rule, but this is intimation of that advice.

*****

A Florida mosque was torched in a case of arson. Donations started coming in, and it was noticed that many were in multiples of $18 - $18, $36, $54. When coupled with the donor names – Avi, Cohen, Goldstein, Rubin, the meaning became clear. Hebrew letters have a numerical value, and 18 is the Hebrew word for "chai" and means "life".

*****

Vandals damaged headstones in a Missouri Jewish cemetery and Muslim activists raised funds for the repairs.

*****

A Christian humanitarian-aid organization was aided extensively by the Israel Defense Forces so that they could provide medical care for Syrian refugees, most of whom were Muslim.

Chapter Four

Leviticus - Chapter 6 - Don't deal with known stolen items.

Leviticus – Chapter 19 – Do not steal.

Deuteronomy - Chapter 5 – And you shall not steal.

Matthew - Chapter 19 - Don't steal.

Surah Al-Baqarah – 188 – Do not consume another's wealth.

Not only shouldn't you steal, but you shouldn't have anything to do with others who do. This also feeds back to the giving information about crimes brought up in Chapter 1. And it doesn't distinguish that some people are ok to steal from and not others. Nope. Just don't do it. Pretty self-explanatory.

Chapter Five

Leviticus - Chapter 5 - Make good on your pledges to others.

Numbers - Chapter 30 - Keep your vows.

Deuteronomy - Chapter 23 - Keep your vows.

When you get down to it, the adultery clause pretty much falls under this. Keeping your vows. If you can't, if you're not sure, if you have trouble with follow-thru, then don't make the vow. Mostly this covers vows you make public. Vows you make to yourself are between you and God, and I'm sure God will track those, and you're probably pretty motivated to keep those. Though I would posit that individuals do practice the wisdom in these religious texts even without the idea of an overseeing authoritarian deity.

Politicians could learn a lot from these phrases. Even the ones who promote their religious background are just as prone as non-religious people not to keep their vows or to make promises they cannot keep. You are not given an out here. You can't later say that you couldn't keep your vow because of certain conditions or people thwarting you. Nope. If you can't keep a vow, then you're wrong to make it.

No excuses. Makes you wonder if everyone who makes a New Year's Resolution is putting themselves in danger of not living up to scripture. There's a measure of humility in this as well as it should curb a tendency to over-promise. It should require a more considered reflection on what you're vowing and reduce the tendency toward boastful behaviors.

*****

Muslims restored a local synagogue in Turkey. They also reached out to Christian groups that had been formerly persecuted. Abdullah Demirbas said, "This is about learning to respect one another and learning to live together."

*****

Anglicans, Catholics, Methodists, Quakers, Jews, Hindus, Muslims, and Sikhs opened up a night shelter in the United Kingdom to help the homeless.

*****

Christians have been aiding and raising funds to help Jews immigrate to Israel. A recent beneficiary of this help said, "Religion is religion. You can believe whatever you want, but if people need help, they need help."

Chapter Six

Leviticus - Chapter 19 - Don't judge people based on their poverty or their wealth - judge them by their goodness.

Deuteronomy - Chapter 1 - Repetition of not using people's social class to sway you in your judgment of their misbehavior.

Psalms - Chapter 1 - Happy is the man that hath not sat in the seat of the scornful.

Matthew - Chapter 7 - Judge not, that you be not judged.

Judging. Sitting in judgment on others. Tough one. We all agree that we shouldn't do this. We all do it. The legal system requires a judge and a jury of peers to sit in judgment on another. As with coveting, it is part of our internal behavioral spectrum. So, why do I include this when I didn't include coveting? If we all agree that we shouldn't judge, yet we do so on a daily basis ("Look how that tramp is dressed!"), why would I include this as a commonality? This gets back to the comments we made about lying. The judging that is brought up here and wrong is the type of judgment that has negative connotations. Also, the type of judgment that is unwarranted or unjustified or "scornful". In particular, the two verses that reference social class. Don't look upon a person of wealth as better or worse a person just because they're wealthy. And vice-versa in regards to poor people. As soon as we're told not to judge, we're told to judge by "their goodness". This gets to the root of the matter. Judge people by who they are.

Judgment is so often negative, superficial, and quick. None of which we should entertain. You wouldn't want people to judge you without cause or evidence. Therefore, you also should not judge others. Our legal system incorporates evidence into judging someone's relative innocence or guilt, so I think that version of judging is not what is being spoken of here.

There is some biological value in making snap judgments. Some studies have shown that we can tell a lot about a person in a very short period of time. It's that "make a good first impression" or the adaptive ability to interpret danger quickly. It's when we rely on those immediate apprehensions solely is when it becomes a problem. Snap judgments can be reinforced by other people's snap judgments and if we just hang around people who are just like us and pretty much agree on a lot of the same stuff, then snap judgments become ingrained judgments. This starts to harken back to the comments about mobs. There's the problem.

If you are Religion A, and you don't know much about Religion B, but you've heard some things about Religion B that you don't like, and then you hang around Religion A people with no contact with Religion B people, you are now judging from a point of ignorance. It all becomes a self-rewarding circular trap. You then don't treat Religion B people right or nicely and then their potentially negative view of Religion A people gets supported. If we don't analyze or recognize our own built-in biases or prejudices or ignorance in how we form our judgments, that's a problem.

Perhaps that's a level of introspection that's asking a lot. Again, this book is about hope. If you see someone of different ethnicity and your first reaction (judgment) is negative, perhaps you should evaluate why you're having that negative thought, especially if this one individual has never done you harm. People should be based on their goodness. How do you know they are good? It's not like they have a sign: "Look at me! I'm good!" You have to meet them and learn about them. Not judging has an inherent message within it that we should get to know one another. Once we do that, the judgment becomes less of an issue.

Chapter Seven

Deuteronomy - Chapter 5 – You shall not murder.

Deuteronomy - Chapter 27 - Don't smite your neighbor.

Surah Al-Baqarah - 084 - Shed no blood amongst you.

Matthew - Chapter 5 - Don't kill.

Why would I include this one? Is this one we can all agree on? As a supposedly intelligent species, we ignore this absolute-lesson regularly.   All three religions agree on this one. If we want to see where we offend God, and humanity generally, this is probably the main way we do it. Individually and in groups and in public settings we shake our heads mournfully and agree that killing is bad. We lament the necessity for war but don't protest about it to the point that it stops. Violence begets violence, and we all seem just to accept it. We're not supposed to be killing each other. And so deliberately too. Religious people also are some of the ones who condone capital punishment; it's a weird bit of cognitive dissonance, yet humans are amazing at holding equally strong disparate points of view. There are certainly a lot of arguments out there. Justifications again. If people were going to take their scripture seriously, however, no one should be killing anyone else. For any reason.

I think if you get right down to the core of the matter, we would all like to live in a world where we don't kill. Where we don't kill like it's some species-related past-time, like baseball. I think we all agree that would make for a better world. A world where we don't devote so much time, energy, and resources to killing each other and devote it, instead, to helping each other. Scripture, in a lot of ways, is trying to get us to express our better natures. We have to willfully ignore scripture and our better nature to do the things we do. Each of the followers of the Big Three does not seem to lament death on each other's part. If Muslim A kills off Jewish B, other Muslims don't seem to raise a fuss about it. And I'm not just picking on Muslims - you can punch in any combination of the Big Three killing each other off, and the same would be true. Not a lot of hand-wringing over the part of the people doing the killing of opposite members of a religion. Guys, it doesn't matter who's getting killed. You're not supposed to be doing it at all.

A lot of killing is done in the "name of religion". I would say that as soon as you kill, you have opted out of being a member of that religion. That's a deal-breaker. The nineteen men who ran planes into buildings in 2001 have often been described as Muslim terrorists. When the killer in Norway was described as a Christian terrorist, Christians took exception to this classification, even though they had been coupling Muslims with terrorism for years. This is a salient point in our discussion because the two above examples were not done by Muslims or Christians, but by terrorists. We need to decouple the religious appellation from these acts. These were deranged individuals who used religion as a justification. They are not of the religion. They proved it through their actions.

Religions get co-opted by violent members who reinterpret sacred texts to justify their misdeeds and atrocities. They need to be universally shunned. None of this half-measure stuff where a man goes on a shooting rampage declaring he's doing it based on Christian scripture and some Christians condemn his actions but see where's he's coming from about Muslims. No! He killed. Not a Christian! A Sunni or Shia who bombs a marketplace of their different sect? Not a Muslim! They've declared themselves as apart from that religion by their actions, regardless of their misguided justification. By not condemning their actions and by not being affronted at how they used the religious aspect as a rationalization for such actions, religious leaders tacitly do a nod of assent to every crazy person out there who is motivated in the same manner.

I think that a lot of the people who kill use religion as a rationalization, though there's nothing rational about it. They parasitize the religion as a tool. They have alternative goals than killing the infidel or the blasphemer. They have goals of controlling others and having power and profess a religious agenda to do so. Many so-called "keepers of the faith", manipulate others into committing monstrous deeds, misleading them, mangling their beliefs into something unrecognizable. Again, members of any of these religions should not tolerate their beliefs being used in such a manner. If the followers of Religion A did not hold negative views of Religion B, then the fanatical and the manipulative would not get a silent tacit agreement if they use the code words of Religion A when blowing up people of Religion B. You would see them for what they are - people who have designated themselves as being apart from any religion, and therefore the majority of the human race, because they break one of the biggest rules: Don't kill.

*****

Over 100 headstones were toppled by vandals in a Philadelphia Jewish cemetery, and many Muslims traveled from other states to help repair them. Tarek El Messidi asked, "....all Muslims to reach out to your Jewish brothers and sisters and stand together against this bigotry."

*****

In Berlin, a Palestinian-born politician and the leader of the local Jewish community joined together to rebuild a synagogue, largely destroyed by the Nazis, and create a multi-faith meeting place. Raed Saleh said, "I wouldn't be a good Muslim if I didn't champion Jewish life in my home city, Berlin.......We want to send a signal that Jewish life is part of German culture. You can only meet hate and discrimination by opening doors and reaching out."

*****

In 1942, two Polish Christian women put their own lives at risk when they set up the Council for the Assistance of the Jews when they witnessed the brutality, oppression, and deaths of Polish Jews at the hands of the Nazis.

Chapter Eight
The "Don'ts"

Leviticus - Chapter 19 - Don't gossip.

1 Samuel - Chapter 2 - Don't talk exceedingly proud or arrogantly.

Zechariah - Chapter 7 - Let none of you devise evil against another in your heart.

Psalms - Chapter 5 - Don't boast, deceive, or practice insincerity.

Proverbs - Chapter 3 - Withhold not good from him to whom it is due when it is within your power to do it. Say not unto they neighbour: "Go, and come again, and tomorrow I will give"; when thou hast it by thee. Devise not evil against thy neighbor, seeing he dwelleth securely by thee. Strive not with a man without cause, if he has done thee no harm.

Surah An-Nur - 027 - Enter not houses other than your own houses until you have obtained the permission of the inmates of those houses and have greeted them with peace.

Matthew - Chapter 5 - Don't be angry and insulting.

Hebrews - Chapter 13 - Do not neglect to show hospitality to strangers.

Many of these verses relate to poor and callous manners. Things that we express toward or about others. We're told not to gossip, deceive, be insincere, angry or insulting. These are all bad behaviors toward each other. We are told not to boast, not to be proud or arrogant. These are the behaviors that depict ourselves in a bad light. These are the reverse of the "Do" sections in subsequent chapters.

You're supposed to help your neighbor (which in this case I always feel means anyone else sharing the world, not just the person next door) immediately if you have the ability; you're not supposed to put it off until later or more convenient time for you. Proverbs often says not to pick fights with others, instead be patient and show self-control. Sure, I'm paraphrasing, but picking fights are what we do now with each other. We look for excuses to fight with other groups.

There are many instances of people who, in leading their own lives, do no harm to anyone else. Some people, sometimes in misusing scripture, find offense in the way those people are leading their lives and become angry and insulting and certainly devise evil against them in their hearts. It's like we have a pathological aversion to getting along. We seem not to be content with letting others be as if we're bored and just want to create some agitation. It bothers us, in some strange manner, to see people who are different than us, being content. Some are not content unless they're causing other people discontent.

Unfortunately, sometimes this is done, in some twisted manner of logic, as a defense of a religious outlook. It is not necessary for everyone to agree with your particular religious viewpoint. Those people over there are doing nothing wrong by not following your religious viewpoint. When you get down to it, the only one you need to be worrying about is yourself and your relationship with God. There is nothing in scripture that says everyone must be converted over to your way of thinking. Sometimes it says to just leave other people alone, as it does here. If you don't like another group or person, for that matter, because of the way they lead their life different from yours, look at it this way: there's someone out there that doesn't like the way you lead your life. Would you want them telling you how to lead your life differently, or having rallies and protests against you, or passing laws that infringe or restrict how you lead your life? No. Naturally, you wouldn't. So, as in the Golden Rule, don't do it to others.

I thought the Quran's comment about staying out

of other people's houses to be amusing. Often, scriptural advice seems to be so obvious that it makes me wonder, as here, if this wandering around other people's houses was a problem at one time. It just seems innocuous amongst everything else, unless something more nefarious is being hinted at here. Perhaps it means to not presume upon others; being polite and not intrusive are certainly good characteristics. When you look at a lot of scripture, it makes you wonder why we need to have an authoritative tome to tell us how to do things right. It's sad that such behavior isn't intuitively obvious to the majority of humans. It's sadder that we have to write it down, and then we ignore it anyway.

Chapter Nine
The "Do's" Part One

Isaiah - Chapter 1 - Learn to do well; seek justice, relieve the oppressed, plead for the widow; let us reason together.

Psalms - Chapter 34 - Keep thy tongue from evil, and thy lips from speaking guile. Depart from evil, and do good; seek peace, and pursue it.

Surah Al-Baqara - 274 - Practice regular charity.

Surah Al-Baqara - 083 - Treat with kindness your parents, kindred, orphans, and those in need.

Surah Al-An'am - 151 – Show kindness to your parents.
Surah Al-An'am - 152 - Speak justly. Take care of an orphan's property until they're old enough.

Surah Al-Isra - 023 - Be kind to parents.

Surah Al-Isra - 034 - Take care of an orphan's home.

Surah Al-Mu'minoon - 004 - Be active in deeds of charity.

Surah An-Nur - 022 - Help your kinsmen and the needy.

Surah Ar-Rum - 038 - So give what is due to kindred, the needy, and the wayfarer.

Matthew - Chapter 5 - Reconcile with others. Turn the other cheek. Give to others and let others borrow from you. Love everybody.

Matthew - Chapter 7 - Whatever you want people to do to you, so do to them.

Matthew - Chapter 25 - Give food to the hungry, drink to the thirsty, clothes to the less fortunate, attend to the sick, and visit the imprisoned.

Acts - Chapter 20 - One must help the weak. It is better to give than to receive.

Hebrews - Chapter 13 - Keep your life free from love of money, and be content with what you have.

1 Peter - Chapter 2 - So put away all malice and all guile and insincerity and envy and all slander.

A lot of repetition, a lot of overlap in this section. Learn to do well, do good, seek peace. A lot about helping people and giving to others, the oppressed, the widowed, orphans, kindred, the needy, the wayfarer, hungry, the thirsty, the less fortunate, the sick, the imprisoned, and the weak. That's a lot of people! If we spent even a fraction of time in attempting to fill this scriptural mandate, we wouldn't have time to steal, lie, and kill each other. I know a lot of people do devote time to helping others, and it's commendable. However, it is also very apparent that even with those efforts there are still a lot of people in need, which tells me that not enough people are working at this. Maybe they're too busy stealing, lying, and killing each other. Can you imagine if we put the same amount of effort into helping others that we do in waging war?

There's a lot here about not lying, which I know we covered earlier, but these verses expand on the subject. It's not just lying, but manipulation of others and insincerity and gossip. What's interesting is that these are phrased in such a way that they fall into the "Do" column. That's another reason I thought these should be included here. Earlier we were told, "do not lie". Here we are told to "keep from speaking guile" to put away malice, insincerity, envy, and slander. This is a more positive slant on it - we're told to act in such a way that we reject the possibility of lying. Which requires us always to think before we speak.

Charity, I suppose, can be included in the helping and giving to others section. The only reason I separated it out is that charity, being charitable, is not only an act of helping others, but it is a mental state as well. Being kind and lenient in one's judgment of others is a form of charity. Forgiving and pardoning others for perceived lapses is a spiritual type of charity. We're also told to be active in charity and do so regularly. Do you start to see how all of these verses link together? Being good and kind to parents is brought up a lot, and I think this is different than the "honor thy parents" clause because being and doing good is supposed to be expressed to all. In some ways, it seems a little strange to me that parents, in particular, are mentioned separately from doing good in general. Doing good to all would naturally include parents.

Many of these verses talk about how to get along with each other better. Reconcile with others, turn the other cheek, and treating others the way you want to be treated. We all tend to be a bit over-sensitive especially when it comes to our religion. We want others to not overreact to things we say, yet become very thin-skinned if something is said carelessly about us or our beliefs. Scripture tells us to be less sensitive. If you follow the logic of what scripture is advocating, being less sensitive means you are less inclined to take offense and therefore less likely to say something negative in return about the other person that they may then take wrongly, perpetuating the cycle of misunderstanding and hurt feelings.

Sharing is promoted here as well. Instead of people lamenting that sharing wealth is institutionalized socialism, they need to look no further than their scripture and see that sharing what you have with others is considered good. You are supposed to share. Your first thought should be to share. Socialism is a government enforced mandate of spreading the wealth, to use the negative code-words of contemporary society. If people worked from scripture and shared in the first place, socialism wouldn't even be a concept. This whole idea of sharing and giving is a good one. Because think about it, if we set a positive example for others, with others, then those people are therefore more likely to share and give as well. This is a cycle that is worth perpetuating. It's the opposite of the perpetual cycle of mistrust and hate that is currently practiced between religions and peoples.

A concurrent thought that is expressed here is in being content with what you have. We are a restless species, and certainly, our striving to improve things in our lives is commendable and positive. That striving tends to help others as well. But if you are striving due to a simple want of "more" and are dissatisfied no matter what you have, that's a problem. I think this verse serves a couple of purposes. First, it's saying that you should be happy with what you have because you could have less. It's also trying to mitigate people's wants so that we aren't infringing on other people's territories, resources, and needs. This also links up with the sharing verses, because if people have something that someone else needs, we should be offering it to those people to help them and also to stave off situations that may force people to feel they have to take what they want.

And though this was in the first verse, I saved it to the end: "Let us reason together." The distrust that we have generated between peoples over all of these centuries of living together cannot continue. Everyone seems to be vying for more for themselves or to oppress and withhold things from others. No one seems to understand that there's an additive negativity that even though you may get what you want by bullying or by force, you've generated bad feelings and sometimes hatred toward yourself or your group or your country that makes it less and less likely to get cooperation in the future, if not outright obstruction from others. If we could just view each other as human beings first, as deriving from the same flawed script, and act together to solve whatever problems arise, we could have progress that benefits everyone. As long as we limit ourselves to our shallow waters and restrict our viewpoints so narrowly, not only will we inhibit others in their goals, but we will also not succeed in attaining ours. It's a simple fact. We have no choice but to share this world. Together.

*****

Muslims helped rebuild a local chapel for Christian residents in the Philippines after it was destroyed in a battle between civil and government forces. Father Michael Ufana said, "This act of kindness from the other side of the world is something we can truly learn from. Don't judge others because they're different. You should love them because they are still our brothers and sisters in this world."

*****

Christians and Muslims came together to produce a document called the Common Word, an understanding that without peace and justice between their two religious communities, there can be no meaningful peace in the world.

*****

A Jewish peer who fled occupied Austria as a child funded the rescue of up to 2,000 Christians from Syria and Iraq as a way to repay a debt when Quakers and Plymouth Brethren fed and clothed him, helping him reach Britain in 1938.

Chapter Ten
The "Do's" Part Two

Leviticus - Chapter 19 – You shall love your neighbor as yourself.

Zechariah - Chapter 7 - Show mercy and compassion to one another.

Matthew - Chapter 19 - Love your neighbor as yourself.

Surah Ali'Imran - 134 - Restrain anger and be forgiving toward others.

Surah An-Nisa - 036 - Do good (towards all).

Surah Al-Isra - 053 - Treat each other in the best possible manner, so there is no dissension among you.

Surah Fussilat - 034 - You shall resort to the nicest possible response. Thus, the one who used to be your enemy may become your best friend.

Surah Al-Mumtahanah - 007 - Allah may grant love and friendship between you and those whom ye now hold as enemies.

Luke - Chapter 6 - Love your enemies, do good to those who hate you; bless and pray for those who abuse and curse you; turn the other cheek; be merciful, don't judge, don't condemn; forgive.

John - Chapter 13 - Love one another.

Romans - Chapter 12 - Let love be genuine. Hold fast to what is good. Love one another with brotherly affection. Live in harmony with one another. Never be conceited. Live peaceably with all.

Romans - Chapter 13 - Love one another. Love your neighbor.

Galatians - Chapter 6 - Let us do good to all men.

Ephesians - Chapter 4 - Let all bitterness and wrath and anger and clamor and slander be put away from you, with all malice. Be kind to one another, tenderhearted, forgiving one another.

Colossian - Chapter 3 - But now put them all away: anger, wrath, malice, slander, and foul talk from your mouth. Compassion, kindness, meekness, and patience, forgiving each other.

1 Thessalonians - Chapter 5 - Encourage one another

and build one another up; encourage the fainthearted, help the weak, be patient with them all; always seek to do good to one another and to all.

Hebrews - Chapter 12 - Strive for peace with everyone.

Hebrews - Chapter 13 - Let brotherly love continue.

We're good for words, aren't we? I mean, as human beings blessed with the ability to speak, we sure like to fill the day up with words. This chapter shouldn't need any further comments from me, yet it does; this chapter, these verses, should be able to stand on their own. I'm sure you can see why I put a chapter two to the "Do" column, since all of these verses, and there are many of them, speak to the same thing, across all of the Big Three - treat each other properly and love one another. Nice words. I'm sure they get trotted out on Sundays and at Mass and in mosques and synagogues throughout the world.

What we don't seem good at is putting these words into action. Within our local community, under the roof of our particular religious meeting place, we may do well putting forth goodwill towards each other. Amongst people who agree with us and with whom we agree we find it very easy to talk about love and peace. But our good intentions are often not broader than that, and our love becomes more conditional the farther people are from us, or the more different they seem to be from us. Scripture is not saying to love "these people who are like you, but not those people". It is intended for us to love and encourage everyone. It's attempting to show us that we all share a common origin and, truly, we are all related as a species. All of the Big Three agree on this one.

Again, religion, in itself, is not the problem. It's when people get involved and allow their personalities and prejudices to color the religion that is the problem. Scripture, as seen in these verses, is very clear. How any follower can interpret things differently has to be a willful act, and in that sense, they are doing their professed religion and the rest of humanity a disservice.

Love is difficult. I get that. It leaves you vulnerable. I think that is also why it's talked about so much in scripture. How do you love people you don't even know? I guess you must get to know them. And that makes us uncomfortable. But you know what? They feel the same way. Their religion tells them to do the same thing, reach out and love others, and it's difficult for them just as much as you. Someone has to yield and drop their defenses. That's the way that love works.

Chapter Eleven

Isaiah – Chapter 2 and Micah – Chapter 4 – They shall beat their swords into plowshares, and their spears into pruninghooks; nation shall not lift up sword against nation, neither shall they learn war any more.

Psalms – Chapter 11 – God hates those who love violence.

This, albeit short, chapter combines elements of the last chapter and chapter seven, the "don't kill" chapter. Just when I think that I have a jaded outlook on life, that maybe mankind can't do better than it does, I read these kinds of words.

These words give me hope.

*****

Muslim volunteers helped provide meals to the homeless at the Salem United Church of Christ so that church members would be freed up to be with their families and attend Christmas services. Pastor Hoerger said the message is about "....oneness and unity. We're all one. That is the deepest place religion can go and, unfortunately, quite often it short circuits getting to that place. Too often religion becomes the barrier to that when it really should be the facilitator." Karen Danielson of the Mosque Foundation said, "Christians and Muslims may observe different customs and holidays, but when it comes to helping those less fortunate, their mission is one in the same."

*****

In Amadiya, Iraq, Christians, Muslims, and Jews coexist. One villager said, "The Jews were always our friends. We never thought about what we were; we were just people living together."

*****

On Scotland's Outer Hebrides, the first ever mosque is being built, thanks to donations from non-Muslim residents.

Chapter Twelve

Psalms - Chapter 4 - Commune with your own heart upon your bed, and be still.

I saved this one until the end. I admit to a little bit of editorial license in doing so, and I have touched lightly on this subject in previous chapters. Your view of life and how you live it is your right as a human being. You may even share a lot of similar views with like-minded individuals. This is a personal decision and journey.

Where we offend each other is when we declare, often quite rudely, that the way we live our lives is the only way and the right way. Sometimes we go on to declare that those other people "over there" live life the wrong way. Then we compound our offense by trying to get them to live life like we do or at least make sure that their way of trying to live is as difficult as possible. That's why I left this for the end. Certainly, there are a lot of things from the previous chapters we all need to work on. But, keeping our opinions and beliefs to ourselves is a step we can all take. Today.

Don't be concerned with what your neighbor is doing or those people at that other church, mosque, or synagogue. Isn't it enough that you try to do right and you and your God have an understanding? We get so uptight about things that are, in the long view, very silly and trivial things. Please read this Psalms verse to yourself one more time.

Epilogue:

I look around the world and see so many problems, many of them, problems that people have manufactured, and I get frustrated at human being's recalcitrant ways. As a fellow human being, it's embarrassing. They say there's no mechanical way to make a Perpetual Motion Machine, one that runs forever on its own, but we have the behavioral equivalent in the troubles we make for each other. And so many of these "problems" are self-perpetuated - "your great-grandfather hurt my great-grandfather, so my grandfather hurt your grandfather, so........etc. etc. etc. You can say that about land too - "my people owned this land 2,000 years ago, and therefore it should be ours and not yours". And how people like to use their particular religious book to prop up their arguments. How much pettier and like a three-year-old do we have to be than to fight over pieces of land? As if we're fighting over our part of the sandbox at recess.

Each individual in the world is responsible for their own actions. Just because you group-identify, doesn't mean that you have to do wrong and inappropriate things because your group does. Be the stronger person - you are only accountable for yourself. Albert Einstein defined insanity as repeating the same things over and over again and expecting different results.

We've been at each other's throats for thousands of years, a lot of it being based on or justified by religion. No one has made any headway or benefited in any substantial degree with these conflicts. How stupid as a species do we have to be to continue in this way?

So, are we stupid or insane? Is there a third choice? I don't think we are an insane species, though there are times I worry that I'm wrong. I don't think we are, because we have such beautiful thoughts and words as seen in scripture that we have written down to prove that we know the right way to behave toward each other. An insane species wouldn't have such a behavioral script to go by. And, in theory, we're not stupid. I think our ego and pride get in the way of how we're supposed to act, but that's different than being stupid. How does this stop?

Well, it stops by people agreeing that some of our actions and behaviors *are* stupid. Let each other be. Let each other believe how they feel they need to believe. Allow each other to live their lives as they deem fit for themselves as long as it is not harming others. Stop judging others by their beliefs. Judge them by their goodness, not whether they pray five times a day, or believe in the Holy Trinity, or have rituals you find confusing. Because I'll bet you they think of themselves as good people, just going about their lives in the best way possible for them.

It requires us to. Just. Stop. Judging.

Wipe the slate clean. Say, "Today, I will start

abiding by the positive aspects of my religion and treating others accordingly. Whatever happened in the past is just that - in the past."

Naive? Well, then I guess God is naive too. Because that's what all of the verses included in this book say to do. Just stop and love each other. Don't let your leaders, whether secular or religious, tell you how to think, if what they say doesn't correspond to loving each other, sharing with and supporting each other, not killing each other.

I think a good litmus test is if your pastor, or imam, or rabbi, or state/country leader uses a specific situation and uses that to refer negatively to a whole group of people, you might want to question that. Especially if they're using it in trying to get your support. Too many stories in our history have been about "getting rid of" or otherwise oppressing a certain minority-people using manufactured fear and relying on the ignorance and blind support of a majority population. Don't let someone co-opt and hijack your religion, or rational thinking, to serve their purposes. Every one of us is responsible for what we do and don't do. We cannot hide within a group or a mob and say we just went along with them even though we disagreed with how they were doing something. Or we stayed silent when someone from our group said things negative and contrary about someone outside our group. We are still individually responsible for our actions and inactions.

There may be some people out there reading these words, thinking to themselves, "Well, this doesn't apply to me. I don't kill people. I give to charity. I help out my neighbor." Great! Good! You're right; maybe this doesn't apply to you.

Perhaps this book could be something you share with others then. Or used as a handy reference, to emphasize the positive commonality of religion and humanity. I'd like this book to make you question if we can do things better or if we can get other individuals or leaders to do and be better. I hope it opens up an internal monologue or even a dialogue with others that explores whether we're doing right by each other in word and deed.

Also, whatever affiliations you may be a part of, do they do things in a positive manner also? Does your state? Does your country? We are all inter-connected and while it's well to do good on a personal level if your country is at war with another, is it based, even in part, for religious reasons? Is it supported for religious reasons? Do you view the "enemy" through the prism of your religion? Considering what is going on in the world today that could certainly be answered as "yes".

Here is the problem. The animosity that religious people bring to the table, this is what needs to stop. This cannot continue and should not be tolerated. It needs to start somewhere. To make changes is difficult but to continue on the same course that we've been doing is just self-destructive. And, truly, we're the ones that make things difficult for ourselves. Taking the view of the Big Three, God/Allah/Yahweh made us. Then He told us to get along. Whenever we don't get along, that is an insult to what God created.

Checking the world population clock, we are just shy of 8 billion people on the planet. About 3.7 billion express beliefs in Christianity, Islam, and Judaism. I'd like to throw in the extra billion people who are non-religious, atheist, or agnostic indirectly. This nearly 5 billion people are who this is directed at mostly, though not to leave anyone out, please feel free to participate.

On the religious side, I wanted a forum in which to show people, who might not otherwise realize, that their religion holds many commonalities with others. I also wanted to make it clear that there are so many scriptural verses that are just common-sense to being a good person. These did not have to be said to us by God or have heavenly punishments associated with them for us to acknowledge that there are right ways to behave with one another.

I've often heard people seem to express that if you are not a religious person, then you aren't a good person. Or, more specifically, if you aren't of their particular religion you cannot be a good person. Religious people do not hold the moral high-ground. There are certainly people who espouse their religiosity who can easily be taken to task for poor behavior and not following their own religion's edicts. This is why I throw that extra billion non-religious people in the mix because the Big Three want to claim that non-religious people can't be good because they don't have the moral underpinnings backed by scripture to do so. It's just another way of dividing ourselves against each other. They're the heathens, the blasphemers, the infidels. Humans like to label each other, especially in the negative column. Well, this is just silly. We're all people, with our flaws and strengths. Condescension gets us nowhere. This is also not how scripture tells us to view other people, just because they don't agree with us or don't believe in the same things in the same way.

I also wish to make clear that you can be a good person and follow the advice that scripture has to offer, without being a religious adherent. You can be a congregant of one. The verses included here should be able to be agreed upon by all as good advice, regardless of their origins. My other point is that a lot of the vocal non-religious people who attack religion need to understand that there is good to be found in it, both for individuals in need and as the propagation of goodwill in the world. Pointing out the hypocrisies that individuals and groups exercise in religion is not positive, nor is it helpful. It is not necessary to attribute a spiritual being to understand that the verses discussed in this book are good ways to approach life. I do understand that non-religious people feel like religion is foisted on them by society and that's to which they're often objecting. Religion is so ubiquitous and religious people so insistent, I understand why some non-religious people push back. It gets back to that topic of finding wrong in others when we should just be keeping to ourselves. Religious people don't like being told there isn't a God. However, other people's non-belief doesn't change what you can believe, so allow them their viewpoint. Just because someone doesn't believe in a higher being, does not negate the idea as a possibility for another. Again, this isn't a matter of who is right or wrong. It is not conducive to understanding for either side to yell that the other is wrong. Not helpful. Not constructive. Not scriptural.

We need to concentrate on the areas that we agree upon, regardless of our backgrounds. Is religion misused and abused? Undoubtedly. Every adherent needs to be vigilant to make sure that their religion is not being used in an ill-manner. When it is, the whole of that religion is painted with the same ugly brush. It often seems to me that the Big Three allow militant and vocal minorities to set the agenda. Then each religion responds to these small groups as if they are representative of the other's religious majority when that is simply not true. They need to be seen for who they are, either misguided people who are misinterpreting what their religion says or people who are just using the religion for their ends. Those who use religion to kill others, oppress others, insult others, are wrong and only serve as a bad example of human-kind.

It was pointed out to me that people of different religions can't get along because their specific religion says they have to believe in a certain way. My argument back though is that how and what you believe has nothing to do with others, it only has to do with you. And if you agree with the verses that have been presented in this book, then the default is that you must treat others well regardless of their own beliefs. If you believe in Religion A, you are still able to have positive interactions with many people, especially when you have no idea what their religion is and if they don't know yours. Since we all hold our own opinion about things, you could probably find several things with which you could disagree with just about anyone you meet. Being religious is only one aspect of being human. You are not defined as just being a member of a certain religion, as if you're all clones of each other. Life is much more complicated than that. Should someone discover, or you tell them, that you are of Religion A, their viewpoint of you should not change because of that any more than the fact that you're an accountant or like the New York Mets. We should not be so fickle with each other. We can't know every nuance and subtlety about one another, and neither do we need to. When you find out that someone, maybe someone who you've had nice interactions with, is a different religion, different political spectrum, different culture than you, does that shade your viewpoint negatively of them? If so, ask yourself why? Because that's not how scripture would tell us to act.

There are a lot of bad people in the world. I'm talking about people that we all agree show an unacceptable level of deplorable behavior. Not just someone with whom we disagree. There are dictators. There are people who subjugate others, who withhold basic human needs from others, who control others, all for selfish ends. There are murderers and genocidal groups. These are people who show the worst side of being human. I have to think that these people continue to be around, in part, because we're so busy fighting among ourselves about religion, about our cultural differences that are informed by our religion, about religious parcels of land, and so forth, that we don't address these truly bad guys. If we could put religion aside as a contention between peoples, maybe we could devote more time to addressing the real problems in the world, not these scripturally-manufactured trivialities.

The only way to do this is to identify each other as belonging to the same species and treating each other properly. Aren't you all just a bit exhausted about pursuing the same stupidities against each other? When you can listen to a news broadcast from forty years ago and not be able to differentiate it from one today, there's a problem. The same over-wrought problems between the same people, over and over again, has to be tiring. I know I find it tiring. We need to turn this around. We need to set a new "normal". If we could take all of the time, energy, and resources that we expend on disagreeing and being disagreeable about religion and devote it toward thwarting warlords and dictators, toward poverty and food distribution and basic freedoms, we might be able to make some headway. A lot of human beings' negative behaviors are brushed off too easily. We excuse someone's outburst or rudeness or short-comings or mistakes as, "Well, they're only human." As if that's a valid excuse.

We need to be better than that. We can't excuse our worst nature as just "being human". We need to cultivate our empathy, our understanding of one another, our compassion. We need to evolve socially and behaviorally, or we have no claim to calling ourselves a higher species.

We have written down how to be good. That is human as well. We know how to be good. When are we going to start practicing what we preach? It's the twenty-first century. It's embarrassing to be a part of a supposedly advanced species who cannot seem to learn such basic lessons. These writings and thoughts have been around for thousands of years. They're not new. Maybe we just need to implement them. I have oscillated from having high aspirations for this book to terrible despair that it's just going to be more words that no one attends to. I know that there are going to be people who will reject this forum for whatever reasons they will give. Even with them, I hope there can be a wedge put into their hardened exterior where a seed can germinate, and these thoughts can grow. I will always have that hope. We need to set aside our pride, our pretensions, and our prejudices. Human beings have such potential. I'd like to see us not continue to squander it.

Shalom

As-salamu alaykum

Peace be with you

Printed in Great Britain
by Amazon

51009278R00050